MANAGING THE SOON-TO-RETIRE EMPLOYEE

KEEPING THEM ON BOARD WITH PURPOSE AND INTENTION

GARY WINTERS

Copyright © 2026 by Gary Winters

All rights reserved.

No part of this book may be reproduced in any form or by any electronic or mechanical means, including information storage and retrieval systems, without written permission from the author, except for the use of brief quotations in a book review.

To Kelly,

The love of my life

CONTENTS

Welcome to Just in Time — vii
About this revision — ix
Introduction — xi

1. When Retirement Looms — 1
2. S-Time to Let Go — 5
3. It's NOT Resistance to Change — 15
4. When Good Employees Go Sideways — 19
5. Why Getting Tough Fails With Sooners — 25
6. First, Redefine the Relationship — 31
7. Then, Recalibrate Expectations — 37
8. Behold: The Check-in — 41
9. The First Check-in — 45
10. Making It Matter — 55
11. A Sooner Speaks Out — 65

Afterword — 71
About the Author — 73

WELCOME TO JUST IN TIME

Management development seminars, workshops, and other formal programs can be terrific investments. But even the best of them share a critical shortcoming–timing.

They rarely occur near the moment when you need to apply what you've learned to a real-life issue. Typically, you attended several months ago, or you aren't scheduled until sometime in the future.

Just in Time books tackle the timing problem with an ever-expanding catalogue of bite-sized books, each focused on a specific challenge, one at a time. They can be read in under an hour.

They're not meant to replace formal training–they enhance and reinforce it.

For a modest investment, *Just in Time* books deliver the insights, techniques, and practical solutions you need–right when you need them.

The book you're considering right now, *Managing The Soon-to-Retire Employee*, focuses on one critical question: How do you keep someone who's got one foot out the door engaged, productive, and committed to the work that still needs to be done?

If that's the situation you find yourself in, find an hour and read this book.

You'll discover why managing the soon-to-retire employee requires a different mindset, why familiar management tools often backfire during this transition, and what to do instead.

You'll see how redefining the relationship, recalibrating expectations, and using simple, purposeful check-ins can help keep a soon-to-retire employee engaged, focused, and contributing—right up to the day he leaves.

In short, this book will help you turn a potentially awkward or frustrating period into one that works—for you, for the organization, and for the employee preparing for his retirement.

ABOUT THIS REVISION

This revised and expanded edition of *Managing the Soon-to-Retire Employee* reflects what has been learned since the book was first published. While the core ideas remain the same, the examples, structure, and guidance have been updated to reflect today's workplace and the realities facing soon-to-retire employees and their managers.

INTRODUCTION

Every day, over 11,000 Americans reach retirement age. Baby Boomers are seeing the end of the line.

The last day of work for most retiring Baby Boomers doesn't happen without some thought and planning beforehand. It's a deliberately chosen date, often determined (or approximated) two or three years earlier.

The planning begins with a growing awareness that retirement is just over the horizon. The employee begins to sense it coming, and soon there's no escaping it. Colleagues and the boss are asking, "So, are you looking forward to retiring? Have you set a date?" Eventually, intentions become clear and the Boomer decides when he will leave the organization for good.

I call employees who've decided to retire within three years or less *Sooners*, because they'll be retiring sooner than everyone else. (I suppose those left behind would be called *Laters*, although I don't use the term in this book.)

In addition, there's a second requirement to be considered a Sooner–the intention to retire must have been made public.

In other words, once someone tells his boss (or his colleagues) that he's going to retire within three years or less, he becomes a Sooner. (By the way, I'll use the male pronoun throughout.)

What's more, once someone becomes a Sooner, he's on "*S-Time.*" Sooner Time. That's the interval between going public about one's intention to retire and the last day on the job.

S-time differs from conventional employee time, because the Sooner now finds his attention divided between meeting his goals and objectives at work, and determining how he wants to arrange his life after he leaves the organization. He has one eye on the ball (his job) and one eye on the future (his retirement).

Therein lies the potential for things to go wrong, because this divided attention might lead to lower productivity, which in turn causes the manager to begin thinking of the Sooner as a so-called "problem employee."

At that point, it becomes tempting to find similarities between Sooners and other employees who will be leaving the organization–those usually called "Short Timers"–the people who've given their two-week notice and are leaving within a few days.

The comparison of Sooners and Short-Timers can seem accurate since they've both made it public that they're leaving the organization and, for the moment, they're still here. Both will find their attention bouncing back and forth between the present and the future. Both *could* become problem employees. But that's where the similarities end.

Short Timers can become a problem because they simply don't care as much as before. And with a time frame that extends only a week or two, there's not much you can do with regard to their behavior other than wait them out–or release them early.

But Sooners are not "Long-Term Short Timers." That is to say, *most* will continue to perform well during their last two or three years, meeting or perhaps exceeding your expectations and continuing to make a positive contribution to the organization.

The fact that they've announced their retirement is duly noted, but remains in the background throughout much of their S-time having little or no observable impact on the employee's day-to-day performance, particularly in the beginning.

It's accepted at face value, but it won't become important again until the last few months when everyone realizes that the Sooner's career is truly coming to an end.

Most Sooners are not problem employees

But some are.

Consider: even if only 5-10% of all Sooners lose their focus and commitment and begin to perform poorly, it means managers across the country are dealing with *thousands* of retiring employees who have problems related to their transition.

And, unlike Short-Timers, they can't afford to "wait out" a troubling Sooner, because two or three years is a long, long time. Also, they can't simply release them early, because these Sooners haven't resigned.

Managing Sooners well begins with a thorough understanding of what it's like to experience S-time–what it's like to be in the midst of a major life transition. Everyone goes through transitions from time to time throughout their career:

- They get married or divorced
- They move to a new home or adjust to an empty nest
- The accept increasing levels of responsibility

What the Sooner is doing is unique. He will complete his transition *outside* the organization and *after* his employment has come to a close.

The difference is significant, and helps explain why managing Sooners presents a unique set of challenges. Dealing with so-called problem Sooners–those who are overwhelmed by their transition–is even tougher. Just as aging isn't for the faint of heart, neither is managing a troubled Sooner!

Sadly, "how to manage the soon-to-retire employee" is rarely, if ever, addressed in leadership academies or workshops.

And, this may be the *only* book on the topic.

One more thing

Toward the end of the book you'll find an "open letter" written by a real-life Sooner, Craig Bronzan, who was facing retirement when this book was written. I asked if he'd be willing to write something which came from his heart about his experience as a Sooner to include in this book, and he agreed without hesitation.

He framed it as an open letter to his boss (actually, to *any* boss). It's included as an honest reflection of what S-Time feels like from the inside. You'll find his letter candid, heartfelt, and insightful.

Let's get started.

1

WHEN RETIREMENT LOOMS

If you want to manage a Sooner well, start by walking a mile in his shoes.

What is it about the idea of retirement that can throw an otherwise competent, steady performer off his game? After all, we have years to imagine it, plan for it, save for it, and decide what we'll do with it when it happens. Of course, not everyone plans as thoroughly as others, but we all know it's coming one day.

When it appears just over the horizon, it starts to become real. It's no longer an abstract concept–it's an approaching fact of life. Soon, the employee *will* retire. With that realization, he begins to talk about it: first with family and friends, then with coworkers and finally, his boss.

At that moment, he enters a special phase that lies between when he's gone public and his final day on the job.

IT'S CALLED S-TIME

During this period, he begins sorting out a set of highly personal challenges that no one around him is likely to be facing.

- *Time collapses* and the future no longer stretches outward; it ends. Decisions start getting filtered through "Is this worth it now?"
- *Attention splits* between essentially two full-time *jobs:* finishing a career and imagining a life that hasn't started yet
- *Identity loosens* as "*who I am at work*" starts to feel temporary, even fragile–sometimes long before performance actually slips
- *Motivation subtly shifts* and external reward (promotion, recognition, long-term projects) lose power; meaning and closure matter more
- *Tolerance for friction drops* as learning curves, reorganizations, new systems, and political nonsense feel heavier than they used to
- *Self-monitoring increases,* as Sooners become hyper-aware of how they're being seen–and worry about being judged as "checked out" or "past their time"
- *Emotions* don't simplify during S-time; they intensify. Pride, grief, relief, excitement, and regret often coexist–sometimes in the same afternoon

Barry, a Sooner for several weeks, finds himself in a meeting about the rollout of a new customer service tracking system. The group is talking about how this will look in three years. It dawns on Barry–he won't be there in three years. The insight takes hold, and he stops asking questions in the meeting. *What will it matter to him*, he thinks, *when I won't even be here to care, one way or another?*

Afterwards, he overhears someone describing him as being 'checked out' at the meeting. The comment strikes him as judgmental and inaccurate. Was it accurate on the surface? Yes. But it missed what was actually happening.

From the outside, many of the shifts that Sooners make are easy to misread. A manager may see distraction where there is reflection, resistance where there is discernment, or withdrawal where there is quiet reckoning.

What's actually happening is that the Sooner is distributing his attention, not losing his commitment. He's *dividing* his attention, not abandoning it. Shifts like these can make capable Sooners *appear* to be problem employees, even when their performance hasn't substantially changed.

The Sooner is still doing the job—while *simultaneously* sorting out his future. That double load is invisible to everyone else, which is why S-time is so often misunderstood and mishandled.

To manage a Sooner well, you first have to understand what he is letting go of—and why that process matters. We'll unpack that in the next chapter.

2

S-TIME TO LET GO

Everyone responds to S-Time in his own way–acceptance and grace, indifference, for others, anxiety and denial for still others. Each Sooner must find his own path. And like most human experiences, each journey is unique while resembling that of others. We all have fingers, but our fingerprints are ours alone.

When an employee moves into S-Time, he'll begin to deal with some highly personal challenges that few people in the organization are sorting out. During this period, while preparing for the next chapter in his life, he is still expected by his boss, his colleagues and clients to continue to perform well–as he has for years. For the most part, no one other than the Sooner fully appreciates the pressure of preparing for the future while continuing to do good work in the present.

S-Time can be *exhausting* and *overwhelming*.

Let's take a look at some of what Sooners have to handle. When you speak with enough Sooners, a consensus of universal concerns begins to emerge. Almost every Sooner must grapple with at least the following:

REALITY #1: THE DAYS ARE GROWING SHORTER

Whereas most employees have a career path that stretches far into the future – five, ten, fifteen or even more years, Sooners are beginning to confront a different reality. Time no longer feels expansive. The horizon is visible.

They start to realize that much of what they will do, achieve, and be known for professionally has already happened. This isn't a sudden realization, nor is it always a disappointing one. But it is a reckoning.

For many Sooners, S-Time becomes a period of coming to terms with that fact—sorting out what has been accomplished, what still matters, and what realistically remains.

- They've already done most of what they're going to do
- They've achieved most of what they're going to achieve
- They've made whatever mark they're going to make

Coming to terms with the fact that the days are growing shorter doesn't happen all at once. It unfolds unevenly– some days with clarity, others with resistance or disbelief. And while this realization reshapes how Sooners think about their work, it also changes how they experience *time itself*. The present and the future begin to blur, overlap, and compete for attention.

This is not to suggest that they have *nothing* left to give or *no* continuing contribution to make. Remember, they still have two or three years of service ahead. Anything's possible. But, on balance, their career is just about over. Most will spend a big chunk of S-time grappling with that.

> *But now the days are short;*
> *I'm in the autumn of the year*
> *And now I think of my life as vintage wine*
> *From fine old kegs*
> *From the brim to the dregs*
> *It poured sweet and clear*
> *It was a very good year*

"It Was a Very Good Year," Frank Sinatra

Of course, not *all* Sooners feel disappointed that their career is coming to a close. Some are impatient for retirement because they want to do things they've been unable to incorporate into their lives while working for a living.

Others aren't necessarily impatient, but they're simply *ready* to step down. They've had their run; it's time to move on.

Still others have been gearing up for retirement for quite some time, and have already come to terms with what their career has meant to them.

But it's easy to see how a Sooner may believe his best (professional) days are behind him. It's been said that somewhere in our late forties and early fifties we begin to reconcile the difference between our career and the dreams we once had.

I was in my forties when I realized I was not going to pitch the seventh game of the World Series for the Cleveland

Indians, which would have followed my time as an astronaut with NASA, not to mention my term as President of the United States.

Although dreams like these may have been set aside, more reasonable aspirations have not, and it may only be when we become a Sooner that we fully accept we're *not* going to become a senior vice president, or we're *not* going to set a national sales record, or we're *not* going to get a technology patent on the Next Big Thing.

For many Sooners, there comes a moment when they realize the party is really winding down. The lights are coming up and the chairs are being stacked.

REALITY #2: TORN BETWEEN TODAY AND TOMORROW

Unlike their colleagues, Sooners have to shift their focus back and forth–from what's happening *right now* to what's going to happen *when this chapter ends*. Maybe not every day, but with a frequency that can threaten their sense of balance.

After all, retiring is one of the most profound transitions a person will make, from *I do this for a living* to *I used to do this for a living*. It's parallel to going from:

- living in your parent's house to having your first apartment
- being single to being married
- being a civilian to being a soldier

Sooners are headed somewhere they've *never* been before. It's a transition far deeper and more complex than changing jobs, moving from one organization to another, or even shifting levels of responsibility as you are promoted from employee to boss.

It's important to note: the switching of focus can happen repeatedly–even several times in a single meeting. It can be dizzying. That's how it creates fatigue before performance ever changes.

> "The transition was difficult. It's hard to stop something that you've enjoyed and that has been very rewarding."
>
> Kareem Abdul-Jabbar

Like caterpillars preparing to crawl out of a cocoon that's starting to crack, Sooners have an insatiable thirst to know what lies ahead even as they remain aware that they have day-to-day job responsibilities to meet.

REALITY #3: I'M NOT QUITE MY 'USUAL SELF'

It's hard to imagine a Sooner who is not at least occasionally distracted, anxious, irritable, or withdrawn for reasons related to his coming retirement.

But if you stop to think about it, you'll realize that Sooners *can't* be their "usual self" much longer. Their identity as an employee is slipping away like the walls of a sand castle swept out to sea. Replacing one identity with another doesn't come without the dizzying sensation of moving two steps forward and sliding one step back. It's not smooth, and it's not easy.

It's only natural they do not always seem like their usual self, because they're not. They're "betwixt and between" two versions of themselves.

Sooners might feel pressured to wear a mask of "business-as-usual" and hide their feelings throughout S-time. Everyone at work (it may seem) wants them to be, or at least appear to be "normal."

They may think they're expected to create the illusion that everything is just as it's always been. If they have issues related to their approaching retirement, they may have been told these should be handled *after* work, away from the organization.

I heard one boss tell his Sooner, "You'll have the rest of your life to be retired. You can get used to it when you finish here. You only have eleven months to complete your career. Make *that* your focus right now, and get on with the job!"

Remember how exhausting it was to attend a social event where you didn't want to paste a fake smile on your face all evening? Imagine the energy it takes a Sooner to maintain the image that "everything's fine, thank you very much," for months on end. While his guts churn every day as he gets closer and closer to his last day on the job.

REALITY #4: MY BEHAVIOR MAY BE MISREAD

Managers watch for early signs that employee performance or commitment might be slipping. It's a big part of their job–it's in their DNA.

When they apply those analytical skills to Sooners, however, they could be making an honest mistake. During

S-Time, common Sooner behaviors resemble the very warning signals managers have been trained to notice.

When a Sooner becomes more selective about how he spends his time, hesitates to invest energy in long-range initiatives, or questions whether a new effort is worth the disruption, a manager may conclude that something is wrong. What feels like good judgment to the Sooner can look like disengagement to his boss.

The manager isn't wrong to notice the change. His mistake could be in how he interprets the change–and what steps he takes next.

REALITY #5: THE ROOM HAS GOTTEN YOUNGER

> *"There was no respect for youth when I was young, and now that I am old, there is no respect for age. I missed it coming and going."*
>
> J.B. Priestly, English novelist and playwright

There's a good chance that a Sooner's peers–and even his boss– are younger than he is. This shift can lead to a sense of isolation and misunderstandings about values, expectations, and even how one should communicate.

For the Sooner, it can feel like it happened overnight. Suddenly, *everyone* who used to be older now looks like they should be in college–if that.

Gone are the judges, police officers, school principals, clergy, pilots, and personal physicians, to name a few, who are older than the Sooner. Gone are the people he instinctively respected because they had lived longer, seen more, and earned their standing through time.

They've vanished, replaced by people who feel so young, they should be the kids on the lawn you want to shake a fist at and yell, "Get off my lawn!"

It's not easy to live in a world where nearly everyone around you is younger. Sooners are startled when they discover that many of the people they work with don't really remember 9/11 or the space shuttle disaster–let alone *ancient history* like Viet Nam or Watergate.

What once felt like a shared story is no longer shared. And that gap can quietly deepen a sense of being out of place, even when relationships are otherwise cordial and work is going well.

SO BEFORE YOU DRAW CONCLUSIONS

As you now know, Sooners are different from other employees in important ways—but those differences are easy to misunderstand. The behaviors that surface during S-Time often resemble the very warning signs managers are trained to watch for: distraction, hesitation, withdrawal, or resistance.

The risk is not in noticing these changes. *The risk is in explaining them too quickly.*

A Sooner amid a major life transition, coming to terms with a finite career, or feeling surrounded by younger coworkers, may look like a performance problem waiting to happen.

In reality, he's doing the difficult internal work required to leave well.

Before taking corrective action, you must understand what's actually driving the behavior you're seeing. Otherwise, you might turn a capable, committed employee into a disengaged one–completely unintentionally.

Now that you understand what Sooners are carrying with them into work each day, we need to look at *how they cope—* and how managers can respond in ways that help rather than harm. In the next chapter, we'll explore the three phases of transition.

3

IT'S NOT RESISTANCE TO CHANGE

> "All changes, even the most longed for, have their melancholy; for what we leave behind us is a part of ourselves; we must die to one life before we can enter another."
>
> Anatole France, French poet and novelist

If there's a predominant stereotype about older employees getting ready to retire, it's that they are resistant to change. Whether it's a new work schedule, or a new technology, or a new policy or procedure, Sooners are often accused of being averse to *anything* that's different from the way things have been until now. This resistance is typically explained as a function of age.

But what's being labeled as resistance is often something else. As Sooners near the end of their careers, many become more selective about which learning curves, adjustments, and disruptions are truly worth the cost *this late in the game.*

The problem is that the stereotype that Sooners are resistant to change is so pervasive that *any* pushback leads managers to believe they have become problem employees.

To understand why this is unwarranted, it helps to examine the reasons people (in general) might resist change. Begin with this notion: it's not that *people resist change.* It's more accurate to say that people resist *being* changed.

Resistance is rarely a knee-jerk response when something new is introduced in the workplace. It's not automatic.

Instead, what we call resistance is a logical extension of a legitimate concern. Here's a list of credible reasons people – Sooners and others – *might* "resist" a change:

- The change is dramatically different from what's happening now. People become *cautious*
- The change is sprung on people with little time for them to think about it before it happens. *Surprise* is inevitable
- The change could result in a loss of face, if it suggests that what went before was done poorly. People don't want to be *embarrassed*
- The change could mean additional work, at least in the beginning. Few welcome that
- There will be genuine losses as a result of the change. People sense they will have to give something up and *grieve it*
- There are too many changes happening simultaneously. Few people enjoy being *overwhelmed*
- *It is being imposed by others with little input or inclusion of those affected by it.* Include me in the planning and implementation of the change and I'll

> likely support it. Impose it on me and I might sabotage it

Believing that a Sooner's so-called resistance is a function of his age is to discount his experience. He may very well oppose something he knows is likely to fail simply because he's seen it fail many times in the past.

It can be hazardous for a Sooner to challenge a change initiative, because doing so risks reinforcing the very stereotype he's trying to overcome. Silence, however, carries its own risks.

A client of mine, Phil, was pulling his hair out because his Sooner, Julianne, refused to throw her support behind a new tracking system Phil wanted to implement. "You know how 'they' are," he complained to me one day over coffee. They just want things to stay exactly as they are until they leave the organization, he said. "They can't be bothered to learn something new unless I read them the riot act. Julianne's resistance is wearing me out!"

"Have you tried talking with Julianne to understand her perspective?" I asked. "Do you actually know *why* she's reluctant to sign on?"

Phil admitted his frustration had prevented him from sitting down with his Sooner and having a calm, candid conversation. He was willing to give it a try.

A week later he admitted to me, somewhat sheepishly, that Julianne had a good point–something about how the system couldn't interface with another department. She wasn't resisting because she was older and intolerant; she was skeptical because she had seen where systems like this tend to break down.

Once Sooners sense they're being stereotyped as resistant to change, many begin to self-protect. They become less candid with their boss and their peers, which can cause solid employees to go sideways—and makes managerial toughness not just ineffective, but actively counterproductive.

And this is often where things start to go sideways.

4

WHEN GOOD EMPLOYEES GO SIDEWAYS

One of the most highly acclaimed television series of all time is called *Breaking Bad*. The title refers to a critical moment when someone begins to behave in ways that are starkly out of character–and often judged harshly by others.

Breaking Bad is the story of a 50 year old high school chemistry teacher, Walter White (played by Bryan Cranston), who learns he has inoperable lung cancer and just a few years to live. Not wanting to leave his family in financial ruin, he "breaks bad," leveraging his scientific skills to produce and sell the world's best methamphetamine.

It's time to take a closer look at problem Sooners – those who appear to be "breaking bad." No, they're not turning to a life of crime and it's unlikely they'll be associated with drug trafficking. Their struggles are far more likely–and far more common–playing out quietly during their final months or years on the job.

At a recent workshop, I asked managers a simple question:

"Do you have a problem Sooner? And if so, what's the problem?" Several hands went up immediately.

The first to speak was Jim. "Well," he said, "I think I do. Her name is Laura, and she's an insurance claims analyst.

"She's starting to drive me nuts! For years, she's always been a pretty good performer. I've had very few problems with her in the four or five years I've managed her–until recently.

"Over the past few months, she's handling far fewer claims than she used to. Mind you, the quality of her work hasn't declined–she's just doing much less of it, at a noticeably slower pace. It's hard not to conclude that she's distracted and her mind is somewhere else. When I've casually brought this up, she gets defensive.

"The only significant change is that she's told us she plans to retire in a couple of years. She's become what you call a Sooner. It was some time after that I noticed a drop in her output.

"I'm not sure how to handle someone with a long track record who has started to slip – especially since she's going to retire soon anyway. She doesn't seem to want to talk about it, and I don't know what to do next.

"But something has to give. When she does less, others have to do more to make up for it. So far no one has said anything about it, but I know they're aware of it. I suppose they're waiting for me to do something. I suspect they're waiting for me to act. But act how?"

Next up was Meredith, who was quite animated throughout her turn.

"I feel your pain, Jim. While the issues I'm having with Charlie are different from yours with Laura, he's another formerly terrific employee who I would swear has undergone a personality transplant!

"He's been around forever. I even looked it up the other day–twenty-one years with the company. He's a purchasing agent. I've always known him as one of the nicest guys on the planet. Lately, he's been clashing with most of the younger or newer employees in the department. It's baffling – and so completely out of character.

It's almost as though he has started to resent the younger staffers simply *because* they're younger. I have no idea where that's coming from!

"He goes out of his way," she continued, "to pick fights with them. He ridicules their interests in the latest technology–smartphones, iPads, all of it. He criticizes them for having an active social life. And he dismisses their ideas on how to improve our processes and work-flow. People have started coming to me to complain about Charlie.

"Honestly, he comes across like the guy yelling, 'You kids! Get off my lawn!'

"Do I have a 'problem Sooner'? You bet I do! Do I know what to do about it? Not a clue. What am I supposed to do–call Charlie in and say, 'Charlie! Stop picking on the kids!'?"

She laughed, but she wasn't amused.

Keith spoke next. "My problem is a guy named Scott, a computer programmer who's spent most of his career in our organization. He's always been as good as anyone at staying ahead of technology changes and industry trends. As I recall, he'll retiring in about two and a half years.

"But lately, something's come over him. Instead of taking pride in being two steps *ahead* of everyone, he's become nostalgic–almost wistful. He likes to talk about "the way things were" so much that people are starting to avoid him.

"I mean, sure, once in a while it's fun to take a trip down Memory Lane. But this is different. It's constant. And the rest of the team is beginning to complain–or, more accurately, they're becoming sarcastic. They'll be the first to admit he has an amazing memory for how things used to be and how programming has evolved, but they also admit that they start to tune out as soon as he begins.

"It's having a real impact on morale and teamwork. And I honestly don't know what to do about him. I just wish he'd snap out of it."

"Amen to that," said Dennis. "I've got a guy, Joe, who is a city planner. Lord knows he's one of the best I've seen. Been with three different cities, each time with greater responsibility and bigger projects.

"Now he's a regionally recognized expert in his field. He's often invited to deliver presentations to professional groups like the League of Cities.

"My problem is that as Joe's expertise has grown, so has his need to remind everyone of it–my staff, outside contractors, private citizens, you name it. Few dispute Joe's expertise, but they do resent having it put in their face all the time.

"I just found out that people are privately counting the days until Joe leaves the organization. I can't let this go on much longer, but just like everyone else so far, I'm not sure what to do."

"You know," said Howard, "I'll trade you my formerly reliable employee, Grace, for any of the people who've been brought up. She's one of our senior recruiters–with us for eighteen, nineteen years. I have loved having Grace on the team. There was a time when I would have said I'd want her on the team forever. I knew I could count on her support, loyalty, and–most of all, her professionalism.

"Then, she told us she was beginning to prepare for retirement. It's still nearly three years away, but she's starting to make her plans.

"Since then, it's like night and day. Something's change. Grace has become a challenge, and it almost always shows up around change. There was a time when Grace was eager to implement changes that improved our workflow. I often asked her to lead important initiatives.

"But that's all in the past. Now, I can count on Grace to *oppose* anything new. Anything we need to change. For example, just last month I tried to introduce a new resume tagging system, and sure enough, Grace was adamantly against it. She insisted that the way we'd been doing it was working perfectly–even after I showed her that it wasn't.

"It was awkward, particularly as it played out during our staff meeting. I can't say her resistance coincides *exactly* with her becoming a Sooner, but it's unmistakably there now.

"I've reached the point where I'm gun-shy about bringing up any kind of change in front of Grace. As sure as I know my own name," Howard said, "I can bet that Grace will oppose it every time.

"I'd really like to know what to do with her. It's going to be a long three years if I can't resolve this."

At first, these situations look very different. One Sooner has slowed down. Another has become combative. Another has retreated into the past. Another has begun to lean too heavily on expertise. Another appears to being resisting change outright.

But what these managers are describing is not a collection of problem employees. It's a group of long-tenured, once-reliable people reacting—often clumsily—to the reality that their careers are entering their final chapter.

Labeling this behavior as laziness, entitlement, or "resistance to change" is tempting. It's also misleading. And when managers respond with the tools they've always relied on, they often discover—too late—that those tools make things worse, not better.

5

WHY GETTING TOUGH FAILS WITH SOONERS

When managers realize a Sooner's behavior is no longer a minor annoyance—but something that's affecting performance, morale, or fairness—they feel pressure to act. Ignoring the issue feels irresponsible. Hoping it will resolve itself feels naïve.

At that point, most managers reach for the same tool they've used successfully in the past to address performance problems: *formal discipline.*

That's where things get more complicated. Dealing with a problem Sooner can be more difficult than dealing with a typical problem employee. For one thing, a classic management tool—the Performance Improvement Plan (or something similar)—is usually off the table.

A PIP is written by the supervisor, often with the assistance of Human Resources, and formally communicated to the employee. It spells out how the employee's performance must change and describes a series of progressively negative consequences—from oral and written reprimands to suspension or termination—if it doesn't.

PIPs are designed for employees who are believed to have a long future with the organization. They allow a supervisor to clarify expectations, timelines, and consequences.

But if you approach HR about creating a PIP for a troubled Sooner, you're likely to hear a sharp intake of breath, followed by a sentence that includes the words *wrongful termination* and *age discrimination*.

HR's concern is that your Sooner could file a legal claim, arguing that you're trying to push him out of the organization earlier than he planned.

Even if there's no real case, the process will be expensive and time consuming for you and the organization. From that perspective, it can seem easier–or cheaper, or both–to tolerate marginal performance until the Sooner actually leaves.

Translated the message often sounds like this: *"It's too late for PIP with someone so close to retirement. If you can't fix the problem, let's let him finish his career as best he can and move on."*

In the abstract, it's hard to fault HR for protecting the organization's assets. But at the micro level–your level–tolerating poor performance is simply unacceptable.

(And to be fair, painting every HR department with this broad brush would be patently unfair. Some HR professionals are highly skilled at coaching managers on alternatives to PIPs for older employees. If yours is one of them, consider yourself fortunate.)

When managers with problem Sooners realize they can't implement a PIP, many simply throw up their hands. They look the other way. They give up.

Instead they resign themselves to biding their time, waiting for (and perhaps subtly encouraging) the marginally performing Sooner to finish that final paperwork and retire as soon as possible.

This "put up and shut up" approach for dealing with problem Sooners is not satisfying. It's not intuitive, and it's counter-productive for at least two reasons.

1. It sends the wrong message to the Sooner. *"You are no longer going to be held accountable."*
2. It sends the wrong message to everyone else. *"We're all going to look the other way regarding our Sooner's poor performance. The odds are good we aren't going to talk about it, either, so you can expect to see it show up as an elephant in the room before long."*

If you're looking for a recipe for low morale, interpersonal conflict, and lower team productivity, you found it.

But, setting lawsuits aside for a moment, HR has a point regarding creating a PIP for a Sooner. Let's walk through what often happens.

Suppose you *did* execute a PIP for your problem Sooner. How confident are you this *"Do better or else!"* approach will succeed?

Let's ask Mac, a Sooner with nineteen months to go. He'd be the first to tell you he's overwhelmed and distracted as he comes to the end of his career.

He's struggling to concentrate the way he once did. He's anxious and disillusioned, quietly asking himself, *"Was that all there was?"*

But to his boss, who knows almost nothing of Mac's angst, he has become a classic problem employee.

Unsure what to do, Mac's boss tries three approaches, all of them doomed to fail.

1. First, he starts nagging him. Mac ignores him
2. Then he micro-manages him. Mac is irritated, but improves
3. Finally he turns to sarcasm, asking Mac, "Who kidnapped the real you–and when are you coming back?" Mac glares at him

None of these techniques work, of course. Mac responds by withdrawing further and become defensive. His boss reaches a conclusion: *it's time for a Performance Improvement Plan* Someone has to lay down the law.

So he up a plan. *Do this, this, and this, by then, then, and then.* Failure to do so could result in anything from verbal or written reprimands to suspension or even termination. He reviews the plan with Mac.

How do you think Mac responded? Do you suppose he...

(A) He thanks his boss for being so caring and compassionate? He takes the PIP seriously, finds a way to get pumped, and starts meeting the expectations and deadlines?

Or...

(B) He decides his boss is a jerk, and figures out subtle ways to undermine him? He says to himself, *"What's he really going to do if I don't meet the goals of the PIP – fire me? A few months before I retire? Not a chance."*

Spoiler alert: Mac chose (B).

So, if you can't put your problem Sooner on a Performance Improvement Plan, what can you do?

There are many ways to approach and inspire Sooners during their final years with the organization. In the chapters that follow, you'll see that instead of relying on the threat of an embarrassing–and largely ineffective–disciplinary process, you can take a positive and powerful approach with any Sooner, problem or otherwise.

You have a choice.

If you have a Sooner or two you can sit back and see how their final months play out. If you begin to experience substandard performance, you can bide your time, and breathe a sigh of relief when they finally go.

Or, you can be proactive. You can partner with them in the first phase of their transition–letting go–and empower them to create a compelling final chapter in the story of their career.

6

FIRST, REDEFINE THE RELATIONSHIP

Muhammad Ali could have been speaking to Sooners everywhere when he said,

> *"Don't count the days, make the days count."*

As the manager of a Sooner, you have an opportunity to help him design the final months (or years) of his employment to be a compelling, meaningful final chapter in his career, not just time to cross off a calendar until he's free to go. You can be instrumental facilitating a shift that transforms him from someone counting the days until retirement into someone continuing to deliver a valuable and worthwhile contribution at work, even as he approaches retirement.

It *is* possible for him to move through the first phase (letting go) of his transition from employee to retiree while performing as a highly productive member of your team.

For that to happen, you must stop thinking your job is to fix a potential "problem employee."

You're going to have to become a monomaniac on a mission. Your new mission–should you choose to accept it–will be to *inspire* your Sooner to *achieve his full potential* as a soon-to-retire employee.

And that means redefining your relationship with your Sooner.

Now part of this may surprise you, because redefining the relationship means *you must stop thinking of yourself as your Sooner's boss.*

Instead, from now on, you're his *coach, partner,* and *colleague.*

Hard as it seems at first blush, it's time to drop the power differential and start seeing yourself as his peer who happens to be his manager.

If this is straining credulity, say this over and over in front of the mirror when you dress for work in the morning: *"I'm not the boss of him anymore."*

You're not?

Well, of course, you still are. But right now, a Sooner hardly needs a *boss* to monitor his performance and give him periodic feedback on what he's done well while pointing out what he needs to improve.

He's been at his job long enough to know these things. Even a poorly performing Sooner is quite well aware he's missing the mark but he may have convinced himself that he lacks the skills, the desire or the energy to reverse the trend.

He doesn't need you to be his boss. He needs you to understand what he's going through, stand beside him, believe in him, and remind him from time to time to be the captain–not a passenger–on his ship of fate.

More simply, he doesn't need you to fix him–he needs you to be there for him–and with him–as he writes his final chapter.

Or, as one Sooner described it much more simply,

 "Build me up. Don't beat me up."

All of this may seem a bit too "touchie-feely." After all, you *are* the boss; you *are* in charge. It's your job to say, "Make it so!" and it's your Sooner's job to do just that–no matter what he's going through during his final days as an employee. *When the going gets tough, the tough get going*, right?

If you still feel this way, I have three suggestions:

One: Read the next few paragraphs until I give you a signal to stop, and then close this book (or your Kindle) and set it aside.

Two: Call in your "problem Sooner" for a little chat, and nip these problems before they get out of hand. Deliver your own version of the following speech...

Randy, I've called you into my office because we need to discuss some things I've begun to notice about your performance. For some time now, I've observed (describe the performance shortfall). This is completely unacceptable–and I am a bit surprised I have to mention it at this point in your career.

Now, I know you're going to retire soon, so perhaps that's got something to do with your substandard performance lately. Maybe you're distracted or something. I have no way of knowing.

Well, you may be retiring, but I am still running the department, and our goals and objectives aren't going away. I need you to pull yourself together and get back to the way you used to be–and I need that to happen immediately.

If you're having problems preparing for retirement, I suggest you check with the folks in Human Resources or the Employee Assistance Program. That stuff is outside my wheelhouse. It's up to you to get help if you need it.

But whether or not you avail yourself of these resources, I expect you to pull yourself together and deliver the kind of performance you've been known for. Am I making myself clear?

Now get back to work and make me proud.

Three: See what happens over the next few weeks. If Randy "pulls it together" and starts meeting your expectations, then you were right and I was wrong. Forget all that stuff about being his colleague, partner or coach. All he needed was a firm kick in the butt from his boss and the problem is "fixed."

Okay – here's the signal.

BEEEEEEEEEP!!!

Bookmark this page, or turn off your Kindle. Do not resume reading this chapter unless, after a few weeks, you're *still* not happy with Randy's performance. We can pick up right where we left off. No worries. I'm not going anywhere. I'll be here when you return.

You're back?

Good to see you again. We haven't a moment to waste, so let's pick up where we left off, shall we?

We've covered why "being the boss" no longer works. At this stage of his career, your greatest value no longer comes from authority or oversight–it comes from partnership.

7

THEN, RECALIBRATE EXPECTATIONS

Once you've redefined your relationship with your Sooner as his coach, or his partner, or his colleague, it's time to adjust your expectations.

It's time to stop paying attention to what you *don't* want your Sooner to do–perform at the margins–and start focusing on what you *do* want him to do.

As his boss, you were accustomed to evaluating his performance like you'd do with any other employee. You might have been doing that with this particular employee for years.

How could you not be alarmed and puzzled at what appears to be marginal performance? How could you *not* notice these shortcomings, when they seem obvious?

How can you *not* want to address this?

A Sooner may be a particular kind of employee, but he's still an employee, right?

Yes, he *is* an employee. And he's a particular kind of

employee, to be sure. *But*–he's an employee in the midst of a unique challenge–transition *out* of the organization.

And, as you've seen, addressing what you perceive as marginal performance the traditional way with threats and consequences is of little use.

That's why it's so important to adjust what excellence looks like with a Sooner. It's *not* marginal performance + looking the other way until he leaves.

It's letting a new picture emerge of excellent performance as a Sooner.

It's making room for the truth that while he might feel overwhelmed, distracted, or anxious from time, he *can still rebound*–often stronger than before.

There are ways for Sooners to contribute that are *unique opportunities* that perhaps only Sooners are uniquely positioned embrace.

So, rather than seeing him as doomed to marginal performance, you can coach him to redefine what excellence could look like. There's a fascinating world of new challenges that await the Sooner–and *only* a Sooner.

The question becomes: what would it be like if the Sooner, as the athletes say, left 100% on the playing field when he walks off for the last time?

> If you express your skepticism and doubt in others, they will return your lack of confidence with mediocrity. But if you believe in them and expect them to do well, they will go the extra mile trying to do their best.
>
> — JOHN MAXWELL

Recalibrating your expectations means shifting from *I'll believe it when I see it* to *I'll see it when I believe it*.

Once you've recalibrated your expectations, a surprisingly simple approach becomes far more effective.

8

BEHOLD: THE CHECK-IN

You've redefined your relationship with your Sooner. You've recalibrated your expectations. Now it's time to roll up your sleeves and work *with* your Sooner to create a plan for his S-Time.

And, if you'll forgive the pun, the sooner you get started, the better.

You won't need a toolbox stuffed with management techniques to get this done. All you'll be using are different versions of something that's deceptively simple and unpretentious.

It's something you've probably done hundreds of times without giving it much thought.

It's called a check-in.

In its most basic form, a check-in sounds like this:

He: "How's it going?"
She: "Fine. You?"
He: "Terrific! Have a good day!"

She: "Thanks, you too!"

We all do this several times a day. At this level, check-ins are often little more than a social ritual—a way of acknowledging another person's presence without really inviting a deeper response.

But even in this simple exchange, something important is happening. One person pauses long enough to notice another. The other responds. And, often without realizing it, they briefly meet as equals.

That matters.

Because when you're working with your Sooner, equality–not authority–is the goal.

Now imagine the same check-in goes slightly differently:

He: "How's it going?"
She: "Just awful! I was rear-ended this morning on the way to work!"
He: "Oh no! Are you okay?"
She: "Well, I thought so, but now I'm not so sure. I'm thinking of seeing a doctor."

At that point, the conversation naturally deepens. Not because anyone is in charge, but because one person actually *meant* the question.

That's the shift you're going to make with your Sooner.

The key to managing Sooners is to initiate a series of ongoing check-ins that start when you learn they're going to retire and continue until they actually do so.

These check-ins will be much deeper than, "How are you?" but they remain conversations between *colleagues*, not a boss and a subordinate.

The characteristics of a Sooner check-in:

1. You both understand that it is a *dialogue* between two different but equal people, not a *discussion* between a boss and a subordinate
2. You've set mutually agreed ground rules
3. Each check-in is seen as one part of an on-going process rather than a finite event
4. The goal of check-ins is an increased understanding of what each of you is going through–both the soon-to-retire employee *and* the manager
5. It is the way you can work together to create and implement a plan for the Sooner's S-time–one that is worthwhile for both of you.

You will use a *unique* check-in to get things started. It's a bit different from the rest. In that first conversation, you'll explain the rationale for check-ins, get buy-in from the Sooner, establish ground rules, clarify your role, and set a schedule.

It's unique, and we'll unpack it next.

9

THE FIRST CHECK-IN

There's one check-in to rule them all–the Very First One. It's important because it sets the stage for *all* that follow.

You may have noticed this chapter is a bit longer than those that preceded it. That's because it walks through the most critical conversation you'll have with your Sooner.

Note: It's *not* a script to memorize. It's simply an example of how a first check-in might unfold.

1. Share the purpose(s) for check-ins.

Paul, since you've announced publicly that you're going to retire in a couple of years, I would like to establish an on-going series of meetings between the two of us–conversations I call them "check-ins."

I'm doing this to create a space where we can both speak freely about how things are going during your final months here.

I'd like your remaining time with the organization to be fulfilling and purposeful, and, at the same time, I'd like you to be ready for the next chapter in your life when that time comes.

I realize that there may be times when you're distracted or preoccupied with what lies ahead for you on a personal level. I also know you understand that as the manager of the department, I still need you to fulfill your professional obligations for the next couple of years, even during those confusing times.

I'd like to work together to craft a plan to cover the next 24 months—one that will meet your needs and mine. Then we can "check in" with one another periodically to see how it's going and decide if anything needs to be changed.

Note: After this opening you need to be in *listening mode*, paying attention what he says and how he reacts. You should *not* be doing all of the talking!

2. Establish some ground rules.

I have a few ideas about some ground rules for our check-ins. See what you think of these:

- *They scheduled in advance and are considered a priority.*
- *They are confidential (unless we both agree something can or should be shared with someone outside the meeting).*
- *We speak as openly and honestly as we can.*
- *We seek to understand one another's point of view—even if we don't necessarily come to agreement on everything (we might have to agree to disagree).*
- *We won't view these meetings as boss-to-subordinate, but rather as colleague-to-colleague.*

3. Describe in some detail how you see your role in these meetings.

Paul, here's what I can offer you through this check-in process. While I'm not an expert in transition, particularly from employee to retiree, I know enough to know it's not always easy. I've learned that the first stage of any transition is actually an ending—you have to begin by letting go of the present before you can embrace the new beginning.

One day, you'll be redefining yourself as a retiree—a former employee. You'll be letting go of many things that "define" you these days.

Your career no longer stretches out indefinitely—it's coming to a close. Your affiliation with your colleagues, your favorite projects, for that matter, even your workspace is going to come to an end one day. That's a lot to sort out!

I want to help make the last chapter of your career to be among the best. I can help you think out loud about how you want to handle transition-related issues and what you want to do with the time remaining. My intension is to be someone who gives you feedback as you work your plan.

It's a privilege and honor to be your manager. Nothing would please me more than to be of assistance to you as you complete your final months here.

I'm not going to give you too much advice, because I believe what Ben Franklin once said: "Wise men don't need advice, and fools won't take it."

Instead, what I will do is hold up a mirror for you from time to time and make it easier for you to think out loud. During these check-ins, I'll ask questions that start with phrases like, "What do you think of..." and "What would happen if..." and "What are the alternatives?" and so on. The answers, of course, will be up to you.

In other words, I'll prime the pump for an on-going, problem-solving dialogue.

4. Get the ball running.

Paul, given this is our first check-in, I'd like to explore a few things, if you're ready. (Note: if he's *not* ready, this can all be postponed until the second check-in.)

First of all, how do you feel about having these check-ins?

The idea may strike him in any number of ways – pleased, enthusiastic, anxious, confused, impatient, etc. Your job here is to do some good listening and acknowledge how he feels.

Bear in mind you're not putting the idea of check-ins up for a vote or his approval. That's the subtle irony about the whole thing. As his manager, you have the right and authority to call for periodic meetings.

But *within* these meetings, you're not going to participate as his boss. You'll be his colleague.

Can you share how you feel about approaching retirement? Are you excited? Anxious? Looking forward? Surprised it's just around the corner? Unsure how to answer? (Etc.) There's no wrong answer or "politically correct" right answer, by the way.

Again, your job is to listen for understanding.

Beyond (or in addition to) simply doing your job, is there anything else you'd like to accomplish over the next couple of years?

Be aware that Paul may not have an answer for these questions–yet.

5. Get the next check-in on the calendar.

Don't bring the first check-in to a close without scheduling the second. You might consider giving Paul some things to think about before the next meeting. For example, you could ask him questions like the ones that follow. Don't throw *all* of them at him–pick two or three:

- *What does he like best about the fact that he'll be retiring in a couple of years?*
- *What does he like the least about it?*
- *What does he anticipate being the most difficult aspect of preparing to retire?*
- *Are there some things he's always wanted to do, but never quite found the time, that he'd like to make sure he tries before he retires?*
- *Has he thought about any special role that appeals to him during his remaining time? (i.e. mentor, trainer, etc.)*
- *Would he like a role training his replacement?*
- *Has he made any plans for what he'll be doing once she retires?*
- *Can he think of anything he'd like you (his manager) to do for him during his last two years?*

A note about whether you're doing therapy

You're not. And you shouldn't be.

If it ever feels like you're doing therapy, call a time-out during the check-in. Let him know that you're beginning to feel that the check-ins are moving too deeply into issues beyond your capacity to be helpful. (For example, a Sooner may want to start sorting out a question of whether he should pursue a divorce as he retires.)

Explain that you feel like you need to be a therapist to be helpful, and that you're not comfortable (or trained, for that matter) in that area.

It's best to refer the Sooner to the Employee Assistance Program, if one is available, or to recommend that they seek the services of a professional counselor, if that's what's called for. You are *not* a therapist, nor should you try to act like one.

That said, done well, check-ins may *feel* therapeutic for both of you, but you should never think of yourself as a therapist for your Sooner.

To do check-ins well, focus on doing just four things:

1. Be a great listener.

You're saying that as the pressure to produce at work increases at the end of the quarter, you're finding it more and more difficult to stay focused because your spouse wants more attention than in the past, is that right?

2. Rather than give advice, ask great questions.

How do you think you'd feel if you...

What do you think the impact of doing that would be?

How do you suppose your spouse would react if you...?

. . .

3. Occasionally, ask about the things that *aren't* being talked about.

I notice that we haven't talked about how this is impacting Sharon and Mike. What do you think is happening there?

I can't remember the last time we've talked about what happened when you...

4. Point out resources that are available.

Have you read Managing Transitions – Making the Most of Change *by William Bridges?*

Did you know the company's offering a 2-hour pre-retirement planning seminar next month?

The many "recipes" for Sooner check-ins

Every Sooner is unique, even though he shares many characteristics and issues with other Sooners. The check-in program for *your* Sooner must be designed and tailored for his specific situation. To help you do that, let's take a brief look at some of the varieties of check-ins. What follows are examples of open-ended questions you might use with your Sooner, if they fit.

They are listed in no particular order. Use them and/or amend them, as you wish.

If the Sooner is feeling apprehensive or not quite ready for his looming retirement.

Are there things you'd like to accomplish before you retire? (If so, what?)

What do you think it's going to be like when you're retired? What about that is worrisome (scary, off-putting, troubling)?

You appear apprehensive about your upcoming retirement. What's behind that?

If the Sooner is having trouble concentrating on his job.

What's distracting you from your work? Could we explore those issues?

What is it about your job that no longer captures your attention?

Are you finding it challenging to stay focused the closer your retirement comes?

If the Sooner is feeling burned out and/or bored with his job.

Do you think you might be burned out? Do you think you'd be feeling this way if you weren't about to retire, or are the two things related?

Can you think of anything that you need to start doing, or do more often, to overcome your feeling of burn-out?

Can you think of anything that you need to stop doing, or do less often, to overcome your feeling of burn-out?

If the Sooner is acting out, sabotaging you, his teammates, and/or the organization.

In the past, I could count on you to (come to meetings on time, for instance). Nowadays, it's anyone's guess when you'll arrive. What's going on? What's behind this shift in your performance?

I'm surprised to learn that you are (being rude on the phone, for example). That's just not like you? What's going on? Is there something bothering you?

While everyone has a bad day or two, or even a bad week, it's very uncharacteristic of you to (fill in the blank). Can you help me understand what's going on?

If the Sooner feels overwhelmed by the challenge of staying focused on his job while preparing for his retirement.

It looks like you're finding it difficult to focus on your job as you edge closer and closer to retirement. Would you agree with that?

When, in particular, are you beginning to find hard to concentrate on the job?

Is there any aspect of your job that you find most difficult to stay engaged with? How does your approaching retirement date interfere with your good intentions at work?

If the Sooner is withdrawing, shutting down, and/or no longer caring about day-to-day activities.

I can't help but notice that you are becoming more withdrawn and quiet lately. Have you noticed this about yourself?

There seems to be a wall you're beginning to move behind. I'm wondering whether you realize you're shutting people out – and if so, why?

This is not like you to project an uncaring attitude about (example). Can we talk about it?

. . .

If the Sooner begins to reflect on his legacy.

Have you thought about what you would like your legacy to be?

If you were to project yourself forward to the retirement event we will doubtless throw in your honor, what do you think you'd hear the main speaker saying?

What are three words that best sum up your legacy? Are you satisfied with those words – or is there something you'd like to do which might lead to different words when the time comes?

If the Sooner wants to do something special during his S-time.

Have you thought about any special challenges you'd like to tackle these days?

You've given much over the years. Is there anything that occurs to you that you haven't done yet that you'd like to be doing now?

If we could rearrange your job by eliminating some of the stuff you normally do to give you time to do some stuff you rarely get to do, what would that look like?

10

MAKING IT MATTER

When managers hear the word *plan*, they often imagine something formal—deadlines, milestones, deliverables. That may be true for some Sooners. For others, it's not true at all.

The plan a Sooner creates for his S-Time is as individual as he is.

A few real examples will make that clear. What follows are not models to copy, but illustrations of how "making it matter" can look.

JAMES, THE ELDER STATESMAN (TIGHTENED EXAMPLE)

Before the check-ins began, James's manager noticed something subtle but concerning.

James was still doing solid work, but he seemed less engaged than he used to be. He no longer volunteered for new assignments, spoke less often in meetings, and occasionally joked about "just riding things out" until retirement. Nothing was overtly wrong—but something had clearly shifted.

Through the check-in process, James began talking about what still gave him energy at work. What emerged surprised no one who knew him well: he loved helping others grow. With about twenty months remaining, James began taking on mentoring assignments—some official, some informal—and quickly discovered how meaningful the role was to him.

Recognizing the value of this shift, his manager adjusted James's workload, freeing up time so he could focus on mentoring newer and younger employees. James became known as the department's Elder Statesman—a trusted guide whose experience was actively shaping the next generation.

James didn't "coast" to retirement. With the right conversations and support, he found a way to make his final chapter matter.

ANTHONY, THE HISTORIAN

As his retirement approached, Anthony was clearly not enjoying his S-Time.

His manager noticed that he had become cross, unusually touchy, and quick to bristle at even minor changes. Anthony didn't want to retire at all. Work had long defined him, and the idea of stepping away left him anxious and resentful.

Through a series of check-ins, that frustration finally surfaced.

What looked like negativity turned out to be fear of becoming irrelevant. Anthony possessed an extraordinary storehouse of knowledge about how things had worked—

and failed—over the years. He had lived through countless initiatives, reorganizations, and course corrections. What he needed was a way to put that institutional memory to meaningful use.

Together, Anthony and his manager created a plan.

Anthony set out to build what he called an "owner's manual" for the department—a document capturing the history behind major decisions, past change efforts, and hard-earned lessons. The plan was concrete and structured, with clear sections, deadlines, and deliverables to ensure the work would be completed well before his retirement.

The effect was immediate.

Far from slowing down, Anthony picked up the pace. Colleagues joked that he had his hair on fire. He met all his regular deadlines while devoting spare moments to the manual. Just as importantly, his demeanor changed. He became more relaxed, more generous with his knowledge, and once again a colleague people enjoyed working with.

Anthony didn't just make peace with retirement.

He reclaimed his sense of purpose—and left behind something of lasting value.

JAY, THE TRAINER

Jay had always been a perfectionist.

For most of his career, that trait served him well. He was highly skilled, deeply knowledgeable, and took pride in doing things the right way. As he moved into his S-Time, however, that same perfectionism began to show up differently. Jay grew more critical of the work others produced and increasingly frustrated when things didn't meet his standards. Over time, his manager noticed that colleagues were beginning to avoid him.

Jay didn't see himself as difficult. He saw himself as caring.

During his check-ins, that disconnect became clear. Jay realized that what he experienced as commitment to quality was being felt by others as constant correction. More importantly, he recognized that what he really wanted wasn't control—it was engagement. He missed the satisfaction of helping things go right.

That insight led to a shift.

Rather than focusing on what others were doing wrong, Jay began channeling his expertise into helping them succeed. He became an unofficial trainer, taking particular pleasure in helping colleagues master the trickier aspects of the job. Instead of pointing out mistakes after the fact, he started showing people how to avoid them in the first place.

The change suited him.

These days, Jay is the "go-to" person in the department when situations get complicated. He's often asked to guide others through difficult assignments, something he does with patience and enthusiasm. The same high standards are still there—but now they're paired with generosity.

Jay didn't lower his expectations.

He redirected them—and, in the process, rediscovered his place on the team

STEPHANIE, THE ROCK

As Stephanie approached retirement, her manager began to notice something that hadn't been true before.

Stephanie resisted change. Not just big changes, but small ones too. A different meeting schedule. A new process. A revised system that everyone else agreed was overdue. Stephanie questioned them all, often with visible frustration. To her manager, it looked like classic late-career resistance—the kind that can quietly stall a team.

Stephanie saw it very differently.

When she reluctantly began participating in check-ins, it became clear that her resistance wasn't really about change at all. It was about uncertainty. Stephanie worked in Public Relations, a department that had been through constant upheaval for years. Reorganizations, shifting priorities, new leadership—she had weathered all of it without complaint. What unsettled her now wasn't change in the organization, but the much larger change looming in her own life.

Talking it through made something else visible.

Stephanie had developed a deep, hard-earned understanding of how people react to change—what helps, what backfires, and what leaders tend to overlook. Once she recognized that this was a strength rather than a liability, her role began to shift. Instead of pushing back, she started sharing what she had learned over the years.

Managers began seeking her out before rolling out new initiatives. Team members relaxed when she was involved. Her calm, grounded presence helped others steady themselves during periods of transition. The very behavior that had once been labeled "resistance" turned out to be insight born of experience.

Stephanie hadn't stopped adapting to change.

She had learned how to help others do it better.

Bill, the Devil's Advocate

Bill had a gift—and it was wearing people out.

As his retirement approached, Bill became increasingly vocal about what wouldn't work. A proposal, a plan, a presentation—Bill could spot the flaw in all of them. He asked the uncomfortable question, pointed out the weak assumption, and highlighted the risk no one else wanted to name.

He was usually right. But over time, his colleagues stopped sharing ideas with him altogether.

Bill noticed. And he wasn't happy about it.

In his check-ins, Bill acknowledged that he felt sidelined. What he hadn't realized was how his constant critique—however accurate—was shutting others down. What emerged in those conversations was something important: Bill didn't want to be negative. He wanted ideas to be better. He wanted the organization to avoid mistakes he had seen too many times before.

That clarity changed everything.

Rather than trying to soften Bill's instincts, his manager decided to formalize them. Bill was appointed the team's official devil's advocate for the remainder of his time with the organization. His role was explicit and understood:

challenge ideas before they were implemented, ask the "dumb" questions, surface the elephants in the room, and stress-test proposals while there was still time to improve them.

The impact was immediate.

Ideas were no longer taken personally. Bill's critiques were expected—and valued. When a proposal survived Bill's scrutiny, it carried real weight. Skeptics became supporters. Even Bill's demeanor changed. He felt useful again.

Bill liked to joke that he'd been given a "license to kill" bad ideas. He even started calling himself 0062.

What mattered more was this: Bill didn't have to change who he was.

He just needed a role where his strengths could finally do their best work.

Susan, the Steady Professional

Susan never looked like a "problem" Sooner.

As her retirement approached, her manager didn't notice withdrawal, irritability, or resistance to change. What he noticed was something else: Susan simply kept doing her job—well, efficiently, and without drama. She didn't ask for new projects. She didn't seek a special role. She wasn't interested in mentoring or legacy work.

Through her check-ins, that became clear.

Susan's plan was simple. She wanted to continue doing what she'd always done: handle her responsibilities competently, meet deadlines, and leave things in good order on her last day. That was enough for her.

Her manager, Hank, adjusted accordingly. He painted the big picture, set priorities, and trusted Susan to execute. There was no need to micromanage. No need to "fix" anything. Susan took pride in finishing strong, and Hank took comfort in knowing one part of his operation required very little attention during a period of transition.

Susan still faced the same questions and emotions that come with preparing for retirement. But she approached them the same way she approached her work—thoughtfully, steadily, and without unnecessary noise.

Her contribution wasn't flashy. It didn't need to be.

For some Sooners, making it matter simply means continuing to matter—right up to the end.

You'll know the level of detail your Sooner's S-time plan needs as you roll out the check-in process. It will be obvious whether it belongs in writing or, like Susan's, is simple enough to be carried comfortably in memory.

That's the management tool you can use to guide your Sooner through this final chapter—the simple check-in.

Initiate an ongoing series of private, confidential conversations in which the Sooner can shape his plan for S-Time. Speak freely, vent, problem-solve, and celebrate progress. Hold a space where he can sort things out, consider options, and decide what matters most.

With someone in his corner who understands the challenges of this transition, a Sooner can thrive—sometimes even surpassing both his own expectations and yours—as he charts a meaningful path from here to retirement.

Don't procrastinate. When an employee makes it public that he intends to retire within the next two or three years, begin the check-in process. Whether he's a steady performer or someone you're starting to worry about, this dialogue should begin when his transition begins.

In the end, you'll both be glad you did.

Everything you've read so far has been written from your "manager hat" point of view. In the final chapter, you'll hear directly from a Sooner–in his own words–about what this transition feels like from the inside.

11

A SOONER SPEAKS OUT

We'll close with an open letter written by Craig Bronzan, a Sooner working for a mid-sized city. I invited him to write this letter because I wanted an actual Sooner to describe, in his own words, what it feels like to be living through S-Time.

Craig was given a general sense of the content of this book, but he did not see any drafts before writing his letter. Any parallels between Craig's comments and the rest of the book are coincidental.

I'd like to thank Craig for his candor and willingness to publish his own story in this book–and to wish him a happy retirement when he finally hangs up his cleats for the last time.

Dear Boss,

"What are you looking at?"

Remember that phrase we used to use when we were kids? That's how I'm feeling right now, ever since I announced my retirement date. It seems like either you want to talk to me about something but you're avoiding me, or maybe you no longer know what to do with me. As I sit here writing this letter I want you to know what while it's true that things have changed, I haven't left. Not yet.

I understand that I have a new classification - I'm a "Sooner" now - someone who's made it public that I'm going to retire within the next few years. Yes, I know I'm am very close to leaving this job, this desk, and this place that has grown so familiar to me. It is where I do what I do. Or, should I say, used to do? The world and my job, my outlook on life, and, to be blunt – my life has changed so much. It's not because I've announced my date. However, surprisingly, telling others the date has made me reflect on a lot of things.

I used to think that my work life was the predictable part of my life. Well, not anymore. As I look back to the place I began, I wonder "how did I get to this place in my life?" When did the amount of sand in the bottom of the hour glass get larger than what is left on top?

I don't think it matters how much you prepare for the day that you say, "Let the countdown begin." Until you get there you aren't prepared. I do not care any less these days, I just care differently. Gone are the days of my youth where outside work activities included sports, games, raising a family, weekends, and the feeling that the good times would never end.

In the beginning I worked to live. And it was fun! Then, one day, responsibility started to catch up with a growing family, aging parents, fractured external family relationships, and bills, bills, and more bills. Work also became more important as I looked for growth opportunities to do more, learn more, and move up the ladder of success. It was hectic but I managed. In fact, I believe I excelled.

As I got older and worked longer, the responsibilities didn't stop; they seemed to become more complicated. Rising health care costs, sending kids to college, being involved in end-of-life decisions for my parents created more in-depth considerations. And the responsibilities in my job increased as more was expected of me, budgets got cut, mergers happened, and the predictability of my work changed – faster and faster. I was asked to think outside the box, do more with less, and would start hearing from upper management that decisions had been made in my best interest.

Funny, I don't remember being asked what my interests were.

So now you're trying to figure out how to work with me as you wonder if I can still add value to the organization. The short answer is, "Yes, I can." However, before you concentrate on the details of the work you need me to perform, you need to understand what this "Sooner" is going through.

I am nearly 60 years old. My body has aches and pains it didn't have when I was younger. My yearly physicals seem to find something new about being old every year. I don't seem to remember things as well as I once did, and my patience seems to be a little thinner. The cost of college, co-pays, prescription drugs, and life in general seems to be going higher – much faster than the returns on my retirement savings. Yes, my personal life has changed a lot. It has a carryover effect on my work life.

However, I bring years of experience, skills and abilities that only time develops. I have been a leader, a mentor, a coach, a dedicated and loyal employee who is now trying to figure out what I will do when I leave this job and the answers to questions that now preoccupy my thoughts. Did I plan well enough for retirement? Are my kids able to make it on their own? Will I really get a second half of life out of this old body? Decisions about what I was going to do for fun this weekend are being replaced with decisions about what the future holds for the second part of my life.

You ask, "Can I still add value to the job?" As I said before, yes, I can. Although the day I walk out of here for the last time is coming quickly, I want to be valued to the very end and add value to what I do. If you want me to add value through the last day, consider these ideas:

- As me what I want to work on. I have always done better when I feel that what I do is important. I know what I do best and providing with an opportunity to do that will help us both.
- Ask me what still needs to be completed before I leave. I have been at this for a long time and I know what still needs my fingerprints before it is passed along to someone else. I know someone else will follow me and with your support, I would like to help pass the torch of what I have been working on to the next person.
- Ask me what I am going to do after I leave here. It is nice to know that the person you work for has an interest in what you do outside of work. Making me feel like you care about my next adventure would be greatly appreciated.

- Ask me for my thoughts on where the organization needs to go. I have been here a long time and have a good understanding of the strengths of the organization. Rarely are employees asked about their thoughts on the future – we usually have to adjust to the changes that many times we don't understand.
- Say "thank you." As I've said, I have been here a long time, mostly because I'm passionate about what I do. I want to make a difference and be appreciated for my efforts. Saying "thank you" doesn't cost anything and if it is sincere, it really does add joy to people's lives.

I appreciate the opportunity to let you know what I think. If nothing else, perhaps a part of me will live on through this letter in addition to the work I have done, and will continue to do, before I leave.

Sincerely,

Craig Bronzan

Director of Parks and Recreation

City of Brentwood, California

AFTERWORD

Managing the Soon-to-Retire Employee is part of the **Just in Time Leadership** series: short, practical guides for managers who want to handle real-world challenges with confidence and grace.

These books exist for a very specific reason. Leadership challenges rarely give you time to study up or attend a seminar. They surface, and they must be handled.

More often, you find yourself thinking, *"I need to deal with this well–today."* That's where a **Just in Time** book fits — clear guidance, a few proven techniques, and enough perspective to steady your footing when the clock is ticking.

If this book spoke to you, you might also enjoy others in the series:

- *Managing Friends & Former Peers*
- *So, How Was Your Meeting?*
- *Help! They Want Me to Be a Supervisor*

Forthcoming titles include:

- *Getting People to Speak Up*
- *Getting People to Hush Up*
- *Building Trust in a Crazy World*
- *Getting People to Stop Triangulating*

More are on the way.

Each one focuses on a single leadership challenge but shares the same tone—conversational, realistic, and ready to use. Together, they form a compact library of timeless skills that help you lead with clarity, consistency, and respect.

If you found this book helpful, please consider leaving a brief review on Amazon. It helps other readers discover the series and lets me know what's landing with you.

You can find more ideas, updates, and upcoming projects at **garywinters.com**, including news about future **Just in Time** titles.

Thanks for reading–and for choosing to grow as a leader when it would be easier to coast. That choice, more than any technique or theory, is what makes you someone others will want to follow.

Warm regards,

Gary Winters

ABOUT THE AUTHOR

Gary Winters is a leadership coach, workshop facilitator, and the author of eight books, including the *Just in Time Leadership* series. His work focuses on practical, human-centered leadership—in particular, the moments managers don't have time to prepare for, but still need to handle well.

The *Just in Time Leadership* books are designed for real-world situations: short, focused guides that help managers think clearly and act confidently when challenges surface without warning.

Gary lives in Vancouver, Washington.

Contact Information

Website: www.garywinters.com

Email: gary@garywinters.com

www.ingramcontent.com/pod-product-compliance
Lightning Source LLC
Chambersburg PA
CBHW070203230526
45471CB00002B/796